# PROTOKOLL

**AN ENGLISH TRANSLATION FROM THE ORIGINAL**

# PROTOKOLL
## [Report]

Of the
## NEGOTIATIONS
## WITH THE
## OPPOSITION MOVEMENT
From July 21 to 23, 1920
in Friedensau

**********

AN ENGLISH TRANSLATION FROM THE ORIGINAL

Published be the three German Unions
of the Seventh-Day Adventists

# TO THE READER

This is a translation of the *portokoll* [or minutes] from the original as it was published in German by the Seventh–Day Adventist publishing house in Hamburg, Germany. The translators have followed the original, as closely as possible, and have given preference also to the meaning of the speakers as recorded, even at the expense of style, correct grammar and syntax.

It has been prepared for the benefit of English readers who may be interested in the origins of the Reform Movement. It records the proceedings of a series of meetings held in 1920 after the cessation of hostilities [World War I] on the occasion of a visit of some brethren of the General Conference in America. Those who had been disfellowshiped because they wanted to maintain the original teachings felt that t was an opportunity to bring a reconciliation between the leaders in Europe and themselves. The brethren from overseas had not been directly involved and there was the hope that they could correct the mistakes of the past and maintain the original teachings.

It should be noted that these minutes record the happenings of but one event in the efforts to restore harmony in the ranks of the Adventists. The Adventists leaders, herein, to the minority as "the opposition." The reader should also keep in mind that these events took place long before the Reform Movement was organized in 1925.

Should additional information be desired concerning these and/or related matters, please send your request to the address below.

# FOREWORD

By publishing the report of the negotiations with the Opposition Movement, we are giving our ministers and church leaders an insight into the course of the discussion as it was held in Friedensau and also the points which arose. The result of the discussion has already been reported in Friedensau as well as in the *Zion's Watchman** No. 15/16 August, 1920

It must be stressed that the protocol should only serve for personal information. We do not wish to stir up the Opposition Movement to new activity in our ranks through provocation. The sooner their matter dies down its own the better. In case of renewed propaganda in our churches, however, use should be made of the contents as be deemed necessary.

It should further be noted that the following deals with stenographic notes of speeches which were impromptu and that the translation from the English was also impromptu. Therefore, although the style and grammar were not always correct, we did not feel that we had a right to correct it in any way, so we let the exact wording stand as it was and also in order not to change the meaning.

R. Ruehling, Secretary

Hamburg, November 1920

---

* [Throughout this translation the name of the German language periodical Zions Waechter will be rendered Zion's Watchman.—EDITOR.]

# Report Of the Negotiations
## with the Opposition Movement
### from July 21 to 23, 1920, in Friedensau

**I. session on Wednesday, July 21, 1920, at 7 o'clock in the evening in the great hall of the new school in Friedensau.**

*Present:* The members o the three German union committees as well as committee members from Holland, Czechoslovakia, Poland, and Hungary, altogether 51 members under the chairmanship of Bro. L.R. Conradi; further 16 members of the opposition movement.

From the General Conference committee, the brethren A.G. Daniells, L.H. Christian, F.M. Wilcox and M.E. Kern.

*Chairman:* Bro. A.G. Daniells.

Prayer was offered by Bro. Wilcox.

As interpreter, first, Bro. L.R. Conradi; in the following sessions, in turns, the brethren M.H. Wentland and W.C. Ising.

*A.G. Daniells:* We have sent for Bro. Ising but will not wait for him as an interpreter and will begin.

We have come together to discuss certain differences in views which have arisen during the war. We have heard of these different questions in America. We were sorry to hear of these different opinions of the brethren in Germany. It is our desire to attain unity and close touch among each other in the whole world. We have not gone into your matter in America so that we have made no decision whatever. We felt that we could not do this at a great conflict and all the difficulties which were connected with it, to go into the matter and to draw our conclusions. We wanted to leave this till we should come here to discuss everything face to face.

Now the time is here, we are here together, and I prayed to the Lord for this gathering. I can tell you all that we have come here without any prejudice in our heart. We have come as brethren of all, and have also a good feeling toward everyone. We are well disposed towards everyone. In our correspondence we did not allow one hard word against one or the other to fall. I often spoke to Bro. Spicer about this matter. He always said this one thing, "We must try to come together, we must try to see matters in God's light and in God's ways." I only wish that Bro. Spicer could be with us. But he only arrives with Bro. Knox in Antwerp on August 4, to take part in the session in Zurich. But we must put ourselves in the Lord's hand and carry on this discussion in the Spirit of Christ and also in the truth.

As you know, I only arrive this noon and was spoke to the brethren of the General Conference committee as to when we could have this session, we agreed to have it as soon as possible. Our time is short, and we thought that as Christian brethren it would be better to discuss beforehand , before we speak to anyone else. There are only three or four persons here with whom I have spoken concerning this, and today I have spoken to no one about the matter. I have also not spoken to any committee in Europe about it. When a brother (from the Opposition Movement) met us in Geneva and wanted to present the matter to us I advised him that we could do it better, not there with one individual, but here, when al are together. Thus we have done all we could eliminate every prejudice in order that we could deal wit the matter in all quietness and justice. A few minutes ago a note was given me (from the representatives of the Opposition Movement) in which they express the request to have a special discussion with the American brethren before this meeting,. But as I have not spoken to a committee before from the other side I thought that we could also let this drop ad discuss the matter here in general.

Now a word about the manner in which we should discuss the matter. The first thing we should have in view is the truth in the matter, to arrive at what is right, not what I think or how I view it, but that which is really right. This is the aim which we should all have in view. This is the thing which takes first place in my thoughts: What is right? What is God's will? And: That we should do His will in this matter. Another thing is the spirit in which we should counsel together. We should counsel as brethren, as such we are. We have a great message which brought us out of the world and has united us. The end is very near. We have only a short time in which to labor to finish the work of God. Therefore, we cannot spend out time quarrelling among ourselves. We must come together in the spirit of mercy, goodness and love. We are all human beings, and in a short time we should either be laid in the grave, or we shall meet the Lord and Saviour, and so we must come together in the spirit of pity and love in order to help each other. I think that is the way in which we should discuss everything.

Now we want to do what is just and good in this matter. We have a lot to do and therefore we must try to be brief, nevertheless we should like everyone to have the liberty to say briefly all that he has to say. Though we are asking the brethren to be brief and only to mentions the main points we do not wish in any wise to take away freedom of speech and I am asking and requesting this of every brother in the house. For those who have nothing special to say it is better to be silent, and those who fell a burden should have liberty to express it. I wish  I knew the circumstances sufficiently to say in which way one could discuss everything comprehensibly point by point, but I am not able to do this. In general, I should like to say that we want to view this matter from both sides. On the one hand, the mistakes tat we think were made, a false judgment that has been pronounced, or wrong course that has been taken, that is one side in consideration; on the other hand, the remedies which we think would help in the matter. I mean the manner, the course and the way we should take in order to remedy the matter. This is something of the way I will propose to lead out in this discussion.

The first thing is not doubt the query as to what mistakes have been made in the affair in question. I think that is all I have to say in the introduction. Naturally I should like to give the brethren who have come (Opposition Movement) the first opportunity to speak, and I expect that you [turning to them] have chosen someone to present your case. I have asked for the whole thing to be taken down in shorthand. It may not be necessary for us to have it written down because it takes a long time but later, if any questions should come up about any point, then we can refer to the report that has been made. But I hope that we shall never need it. And I hope that the Lord will guide our thoughts and hearts that we shall attain to unity in the matter. He is able to do this if we go according to His ways. As far as the past is concerned, the Lord can put that in order. I will tell you what I used to say to young people when they first sought the Lord. They felt a great burden because of their past sins and mistakes which they had committed. They did not see how they could become Christians, and they could also not see how the Lord could accept them because of their sins. But I said to them: It is not the past that troubles the Lord, it is the future for which the Lord has the greatest interest. He can forgive our past sins and make them as white as snow. He ca bring the past in order, and He must do it with every soul whom He saves. But the difficulty is for us to subject ourselves fully and completely to Him so that He can help us for the future. The main thing is for us to come so far that the Lord can help us in the future. The let us pray to the Lord that He may come into the meeting and e the invisible leader of this meeting.

(Bro. Wentland as interpreter.)

*E. Doerschler:* As an International Missionary Society and people, we have chosen a chairman, namely, my humble self during this time, while Bro. Welp answers to the questions for Germany. We are grateful to the Lord to hear such words from Bro. Daniells, and we hope too that the peace of God may be among us throughout the whole meeting. First, I should like to read something. We are standing in this place for the cause of the great God and are in His presence. The solemn responsibilities which we as sinful beings are taking upon ourselves is so great, that we, on the basis of our past experiences cannot do other than to present the followings as conditions. In order that our discussion may be to the honor of God and that our stand towards the law and the Testimony may be clear to everyone, we would ask for an orderly and objective consideration of the principles which come into question, free of both sides from all personal attacks. Should this condition for an objective discussion, which our position before God demands, not be carried out, then it will be impossible to complete our responsible mission. All are fundamental principles which united us as people and have now separated us. We have nothing to do with all the errors which arose since 1914 through the scattering, and refuse any discussion on this point. This is the introduction. Then we have the following main points to mention:

1. What position does the General Conference take concerning the decision which was made by the German leaders

since 1914 in regard to the 4th and 6th commandments. In these points we are referring to the following written declarations. First, the document from the German Union to the War Ministry (he repeats the first sentence after further inquiry from A.G. Daniells, then continues): the following documents may serve as evidences or for discussion. The document to the War Ministry from the German Union, then the document by Bro. Dail in Hamburg, then the tract, *The Christian and the War*, by Bro. Wintzen in Berlin, then the *Explanation* which appeared in the newspaper *Berliner Lokalanzeiger*, from the Seventh-day Adventist leadership, then a document *For Clarification*, published by the leadership. This is the first point.

The second Resolution: What proof can be shown us that we have not taken the biblical course towards the brethren, a reproach which was brought against us in the last *Zion's Watchman* (Z-W. No. 13,14, July, 1920)? (Various inquiries from Bro. A.G. Daniells.) We wish to prove to the brethren that we invited the brethren to a council before. We shall bring this later.

3. What position does the General Conference of the American brethren take towards the Testimonies of Sister White, today. Firstly: are they inspired by God or not? Secondly: Should we continue to proclaim health reform (which she brought to us) as the right arm of the message or not? (After inquiry by Bro. Daniells the preceding words in parentheses were omitted.)

Point 4. Is our message according to Revelation 14:6-12 national or international? We have here various numbers of the *Zion's Watchman* were it cannot be seen that we are an international people. *Zion's Watchman* No. 5, March 3, 1920, page 35, by the school leadership. Our resolutions have herewith been presented, and we would like to ask the American brethren to give an explanation on these questions which have now been set forth point by point.

*A.G. Daniells:* We must have time to examine this in the presence of two brethren from both sides.

*E. Doerschler:* We have a lot of material and would like to put it at the disposal of Bro. Daniells with two of our brethren so that they can examine it. There are many documents. I believe that it would be quite right and acceptable if two from this side and two from the other side were present during the time these documents are being read through. It it is too tiring for Daniells today, we have time till tomorrow.

*A.G. Daniells:* Have you anything more to lay before us today?

*E. Doerschler:* Yes, this is the first mission which we have.

*A.G. Daniells:* If you have other resolutions to present later, I should like to hear them.

*E. Doerschler:* We will present them later.

*A.G. Daniells:* I should like to see the various periodicals and tracts which contain the proofs, It is better to adjourn for this evening.

*E. Doerschler:* It is all right with us.

*A.G. Daniells:* When can we meet tomorrow morning? The time is fixed for o'clock on Thursday morning. Brethren Doerschler and Spanknoebel from the Opposition Movement Party will take part.

Prayer: Bro. Frauchiger. Adjourned.

## II. Session: Thursday morning at 6 o'clock.

Present: The members of the General Conference committee, the German Union presidents, and three representatives of the Opposition Movement.

Prayer: Bro. H.F. Schuberth.

(Bro. Ising as interpreter.)

*A.G. Daniells:* In looking over the list, I find that I have seen most of these documents. The first is the document from Bro. Dail. I have seen that. We do not need to read that again because I have already seen it and know the contents. The session this morning is only for the purpose of looking through the documents which are mentioned. We do not need to look again through the documents which we know. Is this now the documents by Bro. Schuberth which went to the War Ministry, or is there something else? We have already seen that too.

(The tract, *The Christian and the War* by Bro. Wintzen is looked through, especially the parts marked by the Opposition Movement.)

*E. Doerschler:* Can I say something? This tract has been widely distributed and has caused much sensation. This tract has been confirmed in the *Zion's Watchman.*

*L.R. Conradi:* Only Bro. Fischer expresses his approval in the *Zion's Watchman,* but the three Union presidents have already stressed their agreement in the introduction.

*A.G. Daniells:* Is the writer of this tract here? Is Bro. Wintzen present at Friedensau?

*L.R. Conradi:* Yes, but he is sick.

*A.G. Daniells:* To what part (turning to the Opposition Movement) do you object?

Some parts are quoted. Page 18 top part is especially referred to.

This part is as follows: "In all that we have said we have shown that the Bible teaches, firstly, that taking part in the war is no transgression of the sixth commandment, likewise, that war service on the Sabbath is not a transgression of the fourth commandment.

"He who maintains the contrary should bring one single expression from the Holy scriptures or the Testimonies. If he cannot do this then he should beware of making assertions and accusations which he cannot prove."

*E. Doerschler:* This is the conclusion that we get out of this tract.

Further the statement from the *Berliner Lokalanzeiger,* Aug. 23, 1917.

*E. Doerschler:* These and other articles appeared in Germany, and this in particular was published in the largest newspapers. Further, the one from July which is signed by the brethren (the explanation which was given in). Here it is stated that we as Adventists wish to have the same rights as the others who observe Sunday.

Some parts are quoted from the *Explanation.*

*A.G. Daniells:* The next is no doubt the *Zion's Watchman* of July, 1920.

*E. Doerschler:* That belongs to the second point. Before we go over to the second point of the evidences we should like to ask the brother a question. You said yesterday (addressing to Bro. Daniells) that you had not spoken much about it and that you had also given no declaration that you are in agreement with us or with the leaders in Hamburg about the war question. Then something which has been said is not true. It was stated here, namely, that the American leaders shared the standpoint of the leaders here on the military question! (After an inquiry as to when that had been said, he replied: Yesterday evening in the introduction.)

*Spanknoebel:* Yesterday evening he (Bro. Daniells) stated that they had been neutral in regard to the position, but here there is a resolution from the *Zion's Watchman* No, 5, from the year 1916.

It concern resolution 3 of the Hessian conference. It is as follows: "The delegates of the Hessian Conference agree with the biblical position of the leadership of the work in regard military and war service, as being a purely civil duty to which the government, appointed by God according to 1 Peter 2:13,14 and Romans 13:4,5, is entitled.

"The General Conference committee also made allowances for this position at their session which took place in November, 1915, when in rely to an inquiry from the leading brethren of this country, they expressed their standpoint that in this civil matter they grant to the different countries of the world full liberty to adapt themselves to their respective lawful statutes as they had done up till now."

*A.G. Daniells:* Now to the next matter.

*E. Doerschler:* Here now is a list which has been made of heroes in military service.

*F.M. Wilcox:* Why has this list been made?

*E. Doerschler:* I should like to rely. This has been made to show the state how many heroes we have among us and thus to procure a guarantee from the state for the church.

*G.W. Schubert:* Please, proofs for this!

*E. Doerschler:* The proof is obvious.

*G.W. Schubert:* I think that those who made the list must know the motives. These people are continually assigning other motives to us for our actions. They not only do so in this matter but in other things too. We made this list so that we could establish how many of us were in the war and also in order that we might be able to care for the families. We only wanted to have a statistic of how many of our people were in the war and , if necessary, to use it in public because we have been accused very much in public. We have been compelled to do this through the activity of these brethren who traveled here and there preaching desertion. On account of this, we have had many difficulties. Many of our churches were closed because of this, and so we had a list made in order to have something on hand if necessary, to show that we do not belong to those who preach desertion

*L.R. Conradi:* What my motives were and what I desired, and something which Bro. Schubert has not mentioned, is that for 20 years we have been trying to get our young people freed from military service on Sabbath. What I wanted and the reason why we put in the two points was so that this faithful fulfillment of duty might be a ground for reaching the goal for which we were striving in Germany—to get Sabbath off.

*E. Doerschler:* Bro. Conradi tells us that this was to help them reach the goal for which they were striving as far back as 20 years ago. This it is proved that this was done to show the state that we were willing to take part. On the inquiry form especially it is stated: War decorations and of what kind? Bro. Schubert has said directly that we preach desertion, We preached a message, and naturally through this message also, "thou shall not kill."

*Spanknoebel:* We believe that this matter of getting Sabbath free is of human reasoning. But we believe that the Scriptures show us another way to liberty: If the Son therefore shall make you free, ye shall be free indeed.

*G.W. Schubert:* I should like to say something to this.

*A.G. Daniells:* We pass over this. No more arguments.

*E. Doerschler:* In regard to the first point, we have here still an explanation from Bro. Conradi personally, *Zion's Watchman* Dec. 2., 1918.

*A.G. Daniells:* We have now gone through the periodicals which were under No. 1. We wish to see the last number.

The *Zion's Watchman* of July, 1920, is mentioned with the reference that the Opposition Movement did not take the biblical course. They protest against this.

*E. Doerschler:* Already in the year 1915 we invited the brethren to a discussion through this pamphlet. They did not agree to it.

The document by Bro. Richter *Protest against the Advent People* is read which refers to a discussion.

*A.G. Daniells:* That is enough for now. We must have another meeting for a further hearing to give the other side an opportunity of bringing the matter forward too.

*E. Doerschler:* We also some documents for the other two points.

*A.G. Daniells:* What were the points?

*E. Doerschler:* Concerning point 4, we refer to the article of the school leaders in the *Zion's Watchman*.

The article is read.

The sentence by Bro. L.R. Conradi from the article of the school leaders is as follows: "It is a question of learning and showing that our message is not just an English-American one but an indigenous one."

*A.G. Daniells:* What did you want to show by this?

*E. Doerschler:* We want to show what the writer is saying.

*Spanknoebel:* This is from an address by Bro. Conradi.

*E. Doerschler:* We want to show that in such idioms as here there is a national matter. It says here that it is a question of learning that our message is not an English-American one but an indigenous one.

*Spanknoebel:* It is to show that it is not an indigenous but an international.

*E. Doerschler:* It depends here on the translation. It says a national.

*Spanknoebel:* While revelation 14 shows tat it is a message for all, free from all state and national differences, yet a statement such as this turns it into a national matter.

*E. Doerschler:* It is obvious from this.

*G.W. Schubert:* The things he is able to read out of it!

*A.G. Daniells:* What else is there?

*E. Doerschler:* Those are our documents. Here is another, *NO Guile in their Mouth* (this is looked through).

*A.G. Daniells:* Have you now presented the whole thing? When can we meet again as a full committee?

*E. Doerschler:* Let Bro. Daniels decide that.

*A.G. Daniells:* (After a little pause for consultation) What we are saying is that the order brethren should choose speakers and present their matter clearly and then we will discuss it further. Then we will come together at 2 o'clock this afternoon, just as yesterday.

*L.R. Conradi:* Do you wish to leave the reading mater with Bro. Christian?

*E. Doerschler:* Yes.

*Spanknoebel:* We have another request. We attach special importance to the general discussion being short and completely to the point, because all who are here know the truth. Just now the brethren mentioned that we are reading things out of these periodicals to suit ourselves. We have the right to read what we read and the others have a right to read for themselves what they want to read. All we want is to have clear answers to our four questions.

*E. Doerschler:* Then there is NOTHER QUESTION. There was an American brother in Switzerland who wanted to have our *Watchman.* Here are the periodicals. (Bro. Christian takes them.) Adjourned.

**III. Session: 2 o'clock in the afternoon.**

Present: The same as at the first full meeting.

Prayer: Br. M.H. Wentland.

Chairman: Bro. A.G. Daniells.

Interpreter: Bro. W.C. Ising.

*A.G. Daniells:* The committee which was nominated yesterday to examine the documents has been sitting since 6 o'clock this morning. After we had gone through these, we agreed to meet again at this time. We were also agreed that the brethren (turning to us) who represent this conference should give an explanation. In this explanation they should explain the mistakes, whatever kind they may be, of which the brethren are accused. Yesterday, I was very pleased to see the quiet and good spirit in which the meetings were conducted. I think that we should strive to conduct all our councils in a quiet and Christian spirit. It is right and good to mention the facts but we should do so in the right way. Today we should get as far as possible in this matter. We have a great number of members here for a special purpose and it is important for us to make the most of the time. We should not deviate from the purpose of this meeting f we desire to receive a spiritual blessing and we should not concentrate on points of lesser importance. I therefore wish to ask each one of you to help to speed up the matter. The others will now have an opportunity of giving their explanation.

*L.R. Conradi:* As the brethren have asked me to bring this matter before the General Conference committee, I have sought out the necessary documents pertaining to this subject. I will first bring an introduction and then I will take the liberty of laying nine questions before the General Conference. Needless to say, we are extremely sorry that such a thing has happened. If there was ever a time then we should have obeyed the instructions of our Lord and the *testimonies,* to stand together, that time was during the war, even though a difference of opinion of this kind existed. For 28 years we have as people admonished our young folk that they should stay in the country in the interests of the work, and that they should do their duty to the government, that they should bear arms but if possible try to get Sabbath free. We have taken the same position toward those who attended school on Sabbath. No one wanted this position but we have had to submit to the things as they were. When the war broke out a great number of the people acted according to these principles. I was in England when the war broke out. I was not here when Bro. Dail made these statements. I was not here at the time and was only able to contact Bro.

Schubert by telephone, but already on September 21, 1914, I wrote in the *Zion's Watchman* an article about it in which I carefully stated our standpoint and expressed our joy that a great number of our young people had the opportunity of coming together on Sabbath. That was all that they could do under those conditions. On October 19, I quoted a more lengthy explanation fro the Review and Herald in the *Zion's Watchman* and a further explanation to Bro. Spicer from the South America according to our principles which were laid down for our people at that time. On November 2, of the same year, I admonished our members to preach the Word and not to mention political things, and I then took large quotations from the *Review and Herald*. (This quotation from the *Review and Herald* begins with the words, "Thousands today are looking with fear into the future. They are wondering what the end of the present conditions will be and how this great European conflagration may end. What is the meaning of this present situation? S.D. Adventists who feel called to interpret the prophecies are asked by many for answer to this question. Through this, an opportunity which we never had before is given to us to explain to out fellow men the special truths for this time. We could not be doing our duty if we did not take advantage of these golden opportunities today. However, there is a great danger connected with this for us as Christian workers, namely, that we might  be carried away with the spirit of speculation which is at present so rife in the world and might go beyond what the *Holy Scriptures* warrant.") So far I should like to state this as being our standpoint, as far as it lay in our power, up to January 1, 1915. I have a number of documents which further helped to increase our difficulties. A man was imprisoned in Berlin because he himself refused to be vaccinated. Ha maintained that he had certain visions and sent the manuscript to Hamburg for printing, in which he stated that this was the last war, and that the Lord would come before the end of 1915. We did not print this in the *Zion's Watchman* so he had it printed in Bremen. This was the real cause of the difficulty. We could not believe such a vision and could not support it. In a pamphlet, *The Testimony of the Last Church*, Rev. 3:14-22, he began to tell us that the leaders of the work had forsaken the truth. There appeared then, a further pamphlet about the same time in which it was stated to be wrong for our people to buy articles of food. In March 1915 there appeared a further explanation which was from the first man again, and he repeated that we had departed from the truth, and tat the Latter Rain would not fall upon the official church, but on little groups which were outside the church. In April 1915 then followed another publication in Zurich by a certain Herms in which he expressed himself similarly to the first.. The there came a further explanation which stated that the end of the world was at hand. In July 1915 this pamphlet was published in its 100,000 edition and distributed. German law demands that the name of the author and the place were it is printed should be stated. Neither of these were there, but there was a remark on the last page that similar pamphlets could be ordered from the International Tract Society in Hamburg. In my articles I had taken heed to what the *Review* had stressed, namely, that one should not publish such strong declaration at such a time. Because of this pamphlet which was to bring the last message to the world, the police were about to close the house in Hamburg. We further took the liberty of printing the Readings for the Week of Prayer, not for everyone, especially during the war. Sometimes they contained things which applied only to North America. There were eight Prayer readings for 1914 and we only needed seven so we omitted the one by Bro. Farnsworth. We were reproached for suppressing the articles by Sister White. We had no other aim in view than to give our people what was good. Later, we published the whole reading in our periodicals. In the Autumn of 1915 this other periodical appeared in which they sought for a meeting with us. But we were not interested in a discussion because we could not see that it would be good. We were the accused and also the accusers and who should made the decisions? At the same time as these documents were published, the brethren H.F. Schuberth, G.W. Schubert and J.G. Oblander made the following declaration in May, 1915, in the *Zion's Watchman*. (The special parts are read. They are from *Early Writings*. There we read on page 97, "Men whose lives are not holy, and who are unqualified to teach the present truth, enter the field without being knowledged by *the church or the brethren generally, and confusion and disunion are the results*." On page 98 we read, "Those men who are not called of God, and that their labors are very important.") At the same time the Swiss committee: Prieser, father Erzberger and G.W.

Schubert (*Zion's Watchman* of June 7, 1915) gave the following declaration. (It is read.) As these documents appeared in our name, I wrote an article in which I explained the whole matter. Then another man arose who had belonged to us for a longer time, published in 1916 this pamphlet *Signs of the Times* and maintained that in 1914 the end of all things had come. He published further things that we were apostatized, etc. We had visited Bremen several times. We tried as much as possible to restore peace. There were three brethren there who were free as they were working in the ambulance corps. But what we could not agree with was that they had not stated their conviction so openly to the government, but went away from home and into our churches to excite them and maintained that their visions that the end of the world was imminent were from the Lord. We were not to plough the fields; tithe and gifts were to be used to support these people. Then another article from these people appeared in July. We could not let these things stand as they were and as I had been in America at that time (1916) I had met the brethren there. I made a report from there and what I said was that the brethren there had told us that under the circumstances and conditions we had done our best. That was all that I could say. In July 1916 the same Mr. Herms from Zurich had published a declaration in which ha called us Judas and said further, "For forty years these men have tried to estrange us from our earthly fatherland... Dear reader, I ask you, have you ever heard one of these Americans and their helpers praying for the victory of the German arms?" In another place in the same article *The Last Warning Cry* he says, "We have been chosen by God to uphold the right teaching, not an American one." I was an American and I was always accused by these men, yes, they threatened that they would see that I left the country. Then in 1915 there came another periodical from Holland, and in the year 1916 in April, I wrote a detailed report in this little pamphlet in which three points were dealt with and in which the reproaches against our whole denomination were refuted because of personal attacks, etc. In May 1916 old father Erzberger wrote a further article.

In February 1918 a workers meeting of this Movement was held in Cologne. They resolve in this session that service in the Red Cross was "devil service." In a later meeting they explained the former standpoint that only Red Cross service at the front was still "devil service." Because they had drawn up this resolution I was called as a witness before court. Then Bro. Doerschler said - may he excuse my mentioning his name – in the pamphlet *A Clarification* on February 28, 1918, "Because in this world might goes before right, they have succeeded in taking our publishing houses and missionary institutions and still have the impudence to accuse the rightful owners of theft when they use something which belongs to them." In 1918 there appeared a further document by these brethren in which it was stated that the Lord would come in 1918. Here is the reckoning. (It is shown.) In order to make the connection, I should like to say that in 1916 we printed an explanation— we were compelled to, because of these things—ad stated that the great difficulties were caused, not because these brethren had such conscientious doubts, but because they had not expressed them at the right place and at the right time to the church officers. In 1916, not only en were called to service, but men and women had to render auxiliary service. We sent out a declaration in which we gave the assurance that we were willing to do everything, but that we wanted the Sabbath fee. In 1917 we gave a further declaration. After we said that war or peace is still an open question, we repeated that in spite of the movement everyone had complete liberty of conscience, that we would respect each one's conscientious conviction. In the year 1919, there appeared a special number of the *Watchman of the Truth*, 10,000 copies of which were distributed, the title was, *The Apostasy Among the Advent People* with the pictures, *The True Church, the Persecuted One—and the Fallen Church, The Persecutor*. In this periodical they addressed the Advent people. They began with Rev. 15, *Babylon is* Fallen and tried to prove from Sister White's writings that this text applies to us. This *Watchman of the Truth* was not only distributed among our people, but also where we were holding public lectures which were attended by  hundreds and hundreds of strangers, two or three of their colporteurs stood in front of the door and distributed them. In one place they said, "This is the sermon (extract) which Mr. Conradi has held." Several persons heard this and can confirm it, and when they were challenged they said, "You can twist it for the truth's sake." Because they represented us thus, I had to answer and wrote the explanation of 1919, *No Guile in Their Mouth*. There I wrote that they should have stated the truth, and I further briefly summed up the truth and fir the first time gave them and explanation as to how we had come to this conviction. At that time the war was over and I could write several things which I was not able to write before. We received documents from the government marked "Confidential" and we were not able to write these, as well as other things, and therefore I undertook to wait till the time would come when it would be possible. I could here bring further expressions from Sister White which they wrest by saying that they are in their favor. In 1919, there appeared another pamphlet from one of their men, *To all Adventists* in answer to my pamphlet *No Guile in Their Mouth*, and we were called pious rogues. We have never used such language. I also do not need t say that the movement split up and the various parties fought against each other and accused each other of not telling the truth. This separation hurt us, but they organized themselves then, and founded their own unions. Then came the Skodsborger meeting. Moreover, Bro. Spicer was still here in 1917, but no call to the General Conference was made. When I came to Geneva, we knew that you brethren (turning to the Opposition Movement) would now come here, that there would be an opportunity for discussion and (turning to the members of the General Conference committee) for an appeal to you, then this document was printed, in which the former accusations were repeated and in which also the letter of H. Miller of America is quoted and that there are similar reports from 10 states. In was also mentioned in it that that had written to you. The document circulated in all unions and this caused us to mention the matter concerning the invitation here in the *Zion's Watchman* because we believe that wan not right way. Instead of appealing to the General Conference the kept on bringing the conflict into churches. Then we felt ourselves called to bring up the matter in the *Zion's Watchman*. Brethren, I have not been able in the short time to translate our questions to the General Conference into English. (Some questions put by Bro. Daniells are answered, such as, where the headquarters of the Opposition Movement are, upon which Wuerzburg and Frankfurt are given, as well as some questions about that had been previously said.)

*L.R. Conradi:* We have now some questions for the General Conference which I here present.

1. Has our leadership in Europe made a mistake that it tolerated military service by our brethren in peace times as well as tolerated the attendance of our children at school on the Sabbath?

It must be hereby noted that all were desirous of getting the Sabbath free for both parties if possible. Our brethren were in prison for years, not because they refused military service, but in order to get Sabbath free.

2. Under the difficult circumstances, was it right for the leaders of the Opposition Movement to stir up our churches continually, to cause unrest, to tear them down and to found their own churches, although we stressed from the beginning that each individual was free to act according to his conscience and to remain in the churches only they should openly confess their position to the government?

3. Question: Was it right for the Movement to publish pamphlets at such critical time and to distribute them by thousands among the people, that the end of the world will follow, immediately after this war and besides this, instead of putting their own name and publishing house, they pointed to our Hamburg publishing house?

4. Question: Had the Opposition Movement a right to call our brethren, who did military service according to their own conviction during the war, murderers and Sabbath breakers?

It should be noted that our brethren did their best to get Sabbath free or to be of use in the ambulance corps, but through this strong propaganda of the Opposition Movement, they had the greatest difficulties.

5. Question: Had they a right to accuse us of robbing them of their publishing houses and missionary institutions?

6. Question: Had they further a right, without contacting the leadership of the General Conference which was represented here still in 1917, to publish periodicals ad to found their own union, to ordain ministers and to call themselves, *International Missionary Society of the Seventh Day Adventists*?

7. Question: Is it biblical to quote the *Testimonies* of Sister White as they did in their periodicals and then to distribute them among non-Adventists, or are the *Testimonies* only written for the church of God?

8. Question: Had they further the right to distribute the afore-mentioned periodicals, which describe us as the Fallen Babylon, openly to the public after our meetings as though they were quotations from our lectures and in which they use the *Testimonies* falsely for this purpose?

9. Question: According to their report of February 1918 and their session of September 29, 1918, had they a right to take the position that all ambulance service is "devil service" or, according to the altered resolution, ambulance service at the front is still "devil service"?

(These questions are translated into English.)

*L.R. Conradi:* I am sorry, brethren, that such questions are brought up for discussion. They have caused us much pain. Nearly every week we had the police in the house. I was very much hindered because I was an American. Most of our ministers were away and most of our church officers with these things to tear them down.

*A.G. Daniells:* Is this the whole explanation which you wish to give (turning to us) at this time? If so, then we will also take these documents to look through them and to study them. We have now the questions which were put to us from both sides and we should like to give the best possible answers to these questions as early as possible. The brethren think that perhaps this evening at 7:00 o'clock we would be ready and able to give an explanation. Is there any objection to this?

*E. Doerschler:* Does that concern the time or the documents?

*A.G. Daniells:* There is still an opportunity to say something about these four questions and the nine which the others have put.

*E. Doerschler:* We should also like to take our position to these pamphlets. They are not all from us. We have a wish concerning these documents which have been handed in. We should like to examine these in the same way as ours have been examined because there are things here which have nothing to do with us.

*A.G. Daniells:* If it is possible for you to meet with the committee just as this morning, then we will arrange for the same meeting, as now at 7:30 pm and the members from the morning can remain here now.

*E. Doerschler:* We should like to have the sister here who understands English. (This is allowed.)

Prayer: G.W. Schubert.

**Extra Session as a Continuation of the Full Session**

Present: The members of the forenoon session.

Chairman: A.G. Daniells.

*A.G. Daniells:* These are the documents which have been handed to us by Bro. Conradi. They are to show how matters stand with this Movement. We can pick out those which you do not consider belonging to your Movement. The first writing is by Wieck.

*E. Doerschler:* He did not belong to this Movement. I have had the privilege of being with this Movement fro the beginning.

*A.G. Daniells:* How does it stand with the second document by Stobbe?

*E. Doerschler:* Yes, he belongs to us. (No. 3 *The Testimony for the Last Church*, is acknowledged as belonging to them.)

The little pamphlet, *Peace and the Present Truth* is again by the first writer, Wieck. The fifth document, *The Loud Cry*, by E. Herms is again acknowledged as belonging to them.

*E. Doerschler:* I should like to give a short explanation about this. Some people came to us who were very unreasonable. We were not able to tell what kind of people they were and they printed pamphlets without asking the committee because we were not so organized in the beginning.

*A.G. Daniells:* Since when did you begin your organization?

*E. Doerschler:* Since 1915. Just as in 1844, it took 10 years, so now we are able to say that our organization is complete.

*A.G. Daniells:* Did Herms belong to you?

*E. Doerschler:* For a short time. We immediately marked the people when they did this behind our back.

Herms also wrote the sixth pamphlet, *Supplement to the Loud Cry.* The seventh pamphlet, *The Last Message of Mercy to a Fallen World* published in July 1915 without saying who is the author, or the printer, is acknowledged as belonging to them.

*E. Doerschler:* This pamphlet is from us, We acknowledge that it is a mistake that the name is missing.

The eight pamphlet, *A Prayer Reading*, is also published by them, the next pamphlet too. The tenth pamphlet, *Signs of the Times* by Hossfeld is also acknowledged as from them, with the remark that the writer is now disfellowshiped.

*A.G. Daniells:* How long has the man been disfellowshiped?

*E. Doerschler:* It is two years now since he was disfellowshiped?

*A.G. Daniells:* He belonged to the Movement. Did he publish this when he was with you?

*E. Doerschler:* Here again we must say that it was not presented to the committee. He made a time reckoning with which we are not agreed.

*G.W. Schubert:* Who was the committee at that time?

*E. Doerschler:* Bro. Welp and I. I cannot say others, but Hossfeld was not in the committee.

*A.G. Daniells:* Is the man still alive?

*E. Doerschler:* Yes, he was a minister with us, but he is no longer a minister.

*P. Drinhaus:* Who distributed the pamphlet is no responsible writer wrote it?

*E. Doerschler:* The conditions were so at that time: As we were refugees, we were scattered everywhere and it was distributed as in a moment. We said, a part of it is very good, but we are not agreed with the time reckoning.

*G.W. Schubert:* Did you withdraw this in some later writing?

*E. Doerschler:* Yes.

*G.W. Schubert:* Where?

The next pamphlets, some numbers of the *Watchman of the Truth*, are acknowledged as published by them. The further pamphlet No. 14, *The Last Warning Call*, by Herms also.

*E. Doerschler:* After the man is disfellowshiped by us, he has nothing more to do with us.

*A.G. Daniells:* You said you disfellowshiped him. Why?

*E. Doerschler:* Because he did things which were against us.

*A.G. Daniells:* In which way did you disfellowshiped him?

*E. Doerschler:* We met together in the committee and we presented the matter to him but he did not want to see it. Then we said, "it is no longer before us, but before you." [sic]

*G.W. Schubert:* Where there not some shady money matters in connection with Herms?

*E. Doerschler:* Not with us.

*A.G. Daniells:* You brought the man before your committee and pointed to his teaching ad told him that he does not represent your standpoint, and that he is not right also in the matter with the visions which he had had.

*E. Doerschler:* We had no faith in the matter from the beginning. He wrote terrible accusations against Bro. Conradi. That is not right.

*A.G. Daniells:* He was proud and did not accept your counsel and you disfellowshiped him from the church.

The next pamphlet No. 15 is you publication in Holland, also published by you.

*E. Doerschler:* Yes.

*G.W. Schubert:* Had the committee been asked?

The next pamphlet is a periodical published by them in Holland and also belonging to them.

The 17th pamphlet is the minutes of the worker's meeting of September 29, 1918, in which the duty in the medical corps is called "devil service." This is also published by them.

*Spanknoebel:* I was present and some brethren of the committee did not share this standpoint, but the majority voted for it. A short time later it was altered, that is to say, it was dropped completely.

*A.G. Daniells:* Is it therefore so as is stated in the minutes?

*Spanknoebel:* Yes.

No. 18 is a writing by E. Doerschler himself, in which he writes that we had taken possession of the publishing houses and missionary institutes, but that they were the rightful owners of them

*E. Doerschler:* I still take the stand today that wherever the principles were given, since 1844, that is where the publishing houses, and (other institutions) like Friedensau, etc. belong. They belong to the brethren who hold fast to them [the principles].

*A.G. Daniells:* I want to put some questions. First, do you assert that the denomination has taken some institutions which belong to you?

*E. Doerschler:* In as much as they no longer stand for the principles.

*A.G. Daniells:* Your standpoint is that the brethren here (turning to us) have departed from the original principles, and you assert that the organization which you represent holds to the principles and for that reason the institutions are transferred to you.

*E. Doerschler:* We have not yet received an answer to our questions. It depends on what answer the brethren of the General Conference give.

*A.G. Daniells:* All My questions are only for the purpose of becoming quite clear as to what your standpoint is.

*L.R. Conradi:* You have it on you letter headings and papers that you are the denomination which has remained standing since 1844.

*A.G. Daniells:* Do you want to keep this name.

*E. Doerschler:* That depends on the answer to the questions which we have put.

The next pamphlet, *To All Adventists* by Schamberg is acknowledged by them.

*E. Doerschler:* This man also belonged to us but is no longer a brother. He worked for us.

*A.G. Daniells:* How long has he been out already?

*E. Doerschler:* Half a year.

*A.G. Daniells:* Did you disfellowshiped him?

*E. Doerschler:* Just as Herms.

*A.G. Daniells:* Where is he now?

*E. Doerschler:* He is a shoemaker in Krefeld.

The next pamphlet No. 19 *Signs of the Times* by Balbierer containing the time reckoning which goes to 1918 belongs to them.

*E. Doerschler:* The man is here.

*A.G. Daniells:* Is that the man who called on me in Geneva?

*E. Doerschler:* Yes, Bro Daniells can now convince himself that he regrets it today. He wrote it without asking us. But it has not been distributed. It is personal matter of itself.

*G.W. Schubert:* This document has been distributed for a year in the South German churches.

*Spanknoebel:* That is not true. I came into contact with the brother when he was proclaiming this. I showed him his error. He was repeatedly admonished by the committee and thus he had time to distribute these copies. But when the decision was put before him that he should de dismissed as a worker, he let it drop.

*A.G. Daniells:* All these documents have an influence on our work. He still belongs to your Movement. The fact that he has repented does not repair the damage.

*E. Doerschler:* I should like to say a word about this. As long as I know the truth this happened also in former times and before 1914. (I was on various committees.) Those damages also were not made good.

*Spanknoebel:* During the time I was at school I noted down these things myself.

*L.R. Conradi:* The thought came at tat time from Bro. Pieringer who was employed at the school

Their periodical *Watchman of the Truth* is next. Some questions are asked concerning its publication.

*E. Doerschler:* I am the publisher in Holland and Bro. Welp in Germany. We are completely responsible for the periodical.

No. 1, special number, 1919, shows the true and the fallen church on the frontispiece.

*A.G. Daniells:* Are you of the opinion that this picture (the true church) represents your organization, and that the other picture (the fallen church) represents our organization?

*E. Doerschler:* We do not know about America whether they are standing on he old principles or not. But in Germany, unless they withdraw the documents to the Ministry of war, then we form the one picture (refers to the right church) and they the other.

*Spanknoebel:* When we sent this out, other men whom we did not know stood up and said the same. As in Switzerland; we did not know the man.

*E. Doerschler:* Just other word. Some months ago we received a writing from America from a Bro. Miller who has a leading position there, he shares our views fully and wholly.

*A.G. Daniells:* I know Bro. Miller

*E. Doerschler:* There are some pamphlets from Australia.

No. 23 and 24 of the pamphlets were also published by them.

*Spanknoebel:* We wanted to awaken the people to take their position in regard to these questions. It may not have been the right way  but we acted according to our best conviction.

*A.G. Daniells:* In the last writings, you printed the letter from Bro. Miller. Do you know him?

*E. Doerschler:* No.

*A.G. Daniells:* Supposing that he is not quite a sincere character

*E. Doerschler:* We saw in this letter that he too wishes for a reformation among the advent people, and we also realize this, and we cannot judge whether the man is sincere or not. But as he holds a leading position, because he wrote that he was over a field, therefore we supposed that he... (he does not complete the sentence).

*A.G. Daniells:* Supposing,, because Herms took a position against you, you dismissed him, and you rejected Wieck. Supposing, somebody comes and says, you must not accept that as a testimony, they are not sincere people. Now you come and tell us something about the character of these people. Surely you do not want us to swallow the matter before you tell us what kind of people they are. Do you not also think that you should be just as careful in translating such things before you have proved them? If you would come to us, we would tell you several things about this man. At that time, I had to sacrifice a whole day because of difficulties which he caused  the committee. He has not leading position in a field, he was only a minister in Chicago, but he made so much trouble that we brought him before the committee. In most cases, we did not go as far as you did and we did not disfellowship him. We wanted to give him a trial and took him away from Chicago and gave him a further opportunity in another city.

*M.E. Kern:* And the man was so much in favor of the German army that we feared the American state would imprison him.

*E. Doerschler:* We do not want to speak about this. We are sorry that we printed this so quickly and will be more careful in the future.

*A.G. Daniells:* That is what I supposed.

*E. Doerschler:* He lied. He wrote that he had a leading position.

*A.G. Daniells:* All He imagines that he has a high position. He has put himself in this position in his thoughts.

*E. Doerschler:* It has happened with many like that in this Movement, and all has been blamed on us.

*P. Drinhaus:* But also here a difficulty was born and difficulties have their aftereffects, because the pamphlets with the false statements have been distributed by the thousands.

*A.G. Daniells:* I think I understand the situation.

Adjourned

**V. Session. Full Meeting, on Thursday evening at 7:30 o'clock.**

Present: All members of the first session.
Prayer: Bro E. Frauchiger.
Chairman: Bro. A.G. Daniells.

Interpreter: Bro. W.C. Ising.

*A.G. Daniells:* The committee has taken time this afternoon to examine the documents presented by Bro. Conradi, and we have decided that this evening we should come together again to sum up our study and to give our judgment. We have been able to go forward so quickly because the question is not quite new to us. The brethren in America have been able to study the problem of the war in its different phases from the beginning. We were confronted with almost the same problem as you here. It is true that we had another government, a republican one, and therefore the military question was not so marked as with you, but in general our questions were the same as with you here. Then we fid that we are informed of the main points and details of the various persons in general. So we believe that we are just as well in a position to give our judgment this evening as if we would occupy ourselves with it a day longer. There are for questions which were given by the brethren of the Opposite Side if we want to call them so. For reason of expediency we want to say so. We have her nine more questions which are from the brethren of the other side. There are two ways in which we could deal with them. The one way would be to give a brief answer, to say either, "yes" or "no," and if I would accept this plan, we would be finished in ten minutes. Another plan is to clarify the most important principles which are connected with this question and that we explain the questions through the experiences which we have gathered in the course of time. This latter way will take more time. I believe, however, that it will be the better way. We are not a military body, and are not before a court of law. We are here as brethren who want to study the principles more than technical matters. If we say "yes" or "no," then nobody would be satisfied. But if we present the questions before us and consider more closely their underlying principles, then it will be possible for us to come nearer together on this matter. And surely it should be our main desire to come nearer together. This should be our greatest desire. I now want to present the first question which the brethren have submitted to us and that is, 1. What position do the brethren take in regard to the resolution of our German brethren concerning the fourth and sixth commandments?

I can only explain this question clearly when I clarify the general principles of our work. We have found it very difficult to give a general basis in the case of war. The problem is a much more complicated problem than perhaps others which we have. It is not so simple as the ten commandments is exceedingly broad and we are not able to grasp its full meaning, nevertheless we can understand it sufficiently to be able to take a clear position regarding the ten commandments. John says, "God so loved the world…" Surely we can understand this easily. But for the war problem we have no such lines of direction in the Holy Scriptures, as for example concerning our citizenship or the government. Jesus says, "Render therefore to Caesar the things which are Caesar's, and unto God the things which are God's." However, when we study the question of rendering to Caesar the thing that are Caesar's, then we find that this is very complicated. As soon as the war began in Europe we studied the subject carefully in America. Compared with you, we had very great advantages. The war, came suddenly upon you, suddenly, as over night. It surprised you with such rapidity you had to act, to do something, and you could not delay one day. But over there, we had two years time in which to study this question before the war started. On this point, therefore, we had a great advantage over you which made it possible for us to take up a well considered position.

After we had studied this subject carefully however, we found that it confused us very much. We called our most experienced men together brethren Spicer, Knox, Wilcox and his brother, the editor of *Signs of the Times*, brethren Prescott and Thompson, our leading men in America, who occupy the highest positions and have gathered great experience. Brethren, I can tell you that these men found very many perplexing and difficult questions which made it very hard to them to form a decision. It was a question of taking a position upon which all could be united and that was the following – that we as a denomination accept the principles of non-combatants. Non-combatancy was our watchword. This was our position as denomination. We went back to the Civil War in order to confirm this position. Thus our brethren took up this position after long study and discussions. This did not remove all our difficulties which appeared were: What do we understand by non-combatants? What course should a non-combatant take? What part should he take in the war? In what relationship should he stand to the government? If anyone thinks that these questions are as easy as a turn of the hand, the he has not experience in the matters pertaining to the authorities. I should now like to tell you the matter turn out with us. There were some brethren in U.S.A. (I do not mean to say on our committee) who, as soon as we took our position as non-combatants, said: This means that I have nothing to do with the war. I shall not go into the camp (barracks) when I am called up. They did not offer any resistance. When the truck came into the camp, they had to lift them out of it. Then they were given a uniform. The authorities then put them into a cell, but they did not want to make their bed or sweep the floor. They accepted food, but did not go any further. They wanted to fight out their idea of non-combatants and we allowed them. It means that if this was their conviction then well and good. We took the attitude that everyone should act in this matter according to his conscience. Then we had brethren who did not go so far. When they were called up, they went to camp (barracks), but when arrived there, they refused to don uniform. They did some work but they refused to put on the uniform because it was against their views. Upon this they were put into prison and punished. Then we had others who did all except the military drill; only when the gun was handed to them they refused to accept it. They took a broom stick or some other stick and carried out all exercises. That was their conscience and their concept of non-combatancy. Then we had other brethren who went further, taking the gun and performing all military drills that they could do, but they told their officers that they were non-combatants and could not go to the front. Now we have had all the ideas and gradations on non-combatancy. Then we had some brethren who had the spirit of love for their country and they went to the front and fought. They came to England and France and went into the trenches, and I do not know what they did when they were there, but they served and returned when the armistice came. What now was our position towards our brethren with their various attitudes? We have stated that we do not want to conscience for other people. We declared our position as non-combatants. We are not concerned with going to war. We regret the war and are opposed to it. But we must allow every citizen to take his position toward the government according to his own conscience. Not one of these people has been disfellowshiped from our denomination, not one of them has been treated as if he were not a Christian. Our brethren have maintained the spirit of liberty, the spirit of love and forbearance and mercy. We had the feeling that we are not permitted to stand between the conscience of men and the denomination. E believe that we can state certain leading principles, that we can grasp them, but we can not control the judgment of a person. We ca not control his own conviction. We do not believe that we could go so far as to say, "You must not act according to your conviction but according to mine." As soon as you tie up the conviction of another, you take away from him his courage and decisiveness. There is a great danger that somebody who is thrown into prison n the grounds of my conviction and not of his own, will not stand. He will only be able to maintain his position when he stands there on the grounds of his own conviction and his own conscience. So we believe that we would have to exercise the spirit of forbearance and patience with these brethren who had their views on the non-combatant position. However much our own opinions differed on this point in America. There occurred no division and no separation in America. There was not opposition formed through this amongst us. Our brethren are standing together just as they did before the war. The brethren went and came again and we treated them as brethren of a great brotherhood. Although we on the committee or as individual members differed from another in our various views towards the government, yet we felt that it would be the greatest mistake to allow a separation to arise on account of these insignificant questions. I have heard brethren expressing views about the war with which I did not agree, but what should we do in this tie of stress? During the conflict and the war, it was not time for division on questions of conscience and questions of conviction. The brother whose conviction differs from mine is just as conscientious as I am myself. As long as we have no certain limits nor any pronounced rules in regard to our position towards the government, it must be left to each one to act in accordance with his conscience. The brethren in America took the same moderate and tolerant stand as our brethren in Europe. We followed the same course as our brethren in England, France and other countries. In these lands some declaration were given in, which scarcely seems good to us. I should like to say that the declaration by Bro. Dail, when it came to us in America, did not seem right and we regretted this. We received letter from members who condemned it very severely and asked that we should rise and condemn it. We told them that they should be quiet and cautious. This matter broke upon our brethren in Hamburg as suddenly as a windstorm. We could imagine how al our young men in the country would be thrown about in the midst of the great difficulty. We could imagine that the brethren in the leading position in which you found yourselves towards the government here. I should like to tell you what our strongest and best men said. "We would not have given in such a declaration, we would not have it distributed, but during the war e do not want to raise our hand against the brethren who have come into affliction and distress. We want to pray for these brethren, and when the storm is over then let us come together and discuss the matter quietly, but let us avoid every division and split. And thus, brethren, I have never used my pen to publish a condemnation of this declaration, neither has Bro. Spicer. He is non-combatant through and through. And he is also the man who has the courage of his conviction. He has a conviction with regard to the war and would even stand at the mouth of a cannon without moving and inch out of the way. But he said: "Let us not condemn the brethren in Germany and Europe in their distress. Bro. Prescott took the same view. Perhaps some of us exaggerated it somewhat, but I can tell you that he has tolerance, love and forbearance enough not to call forth a separation. And so I could say in general about the document to the war ministry by Bro. Schubert the following: There were expressions in it which we regretted and we believe that if he had had a year's time to think over the matter and if he had had the time to talk with the young brethren, then he would have composed it differently. We had time over there, but in spite of our views which we had concerning this declarations which was given in, we sent no word of reply. We believe that it would be wise to wait till we came over and discuss it face to face, and we did so. And thus brethren when we had the opportunity to come together and see each other face to face, we are in a position to delve deeper into the matter and still to remain together. I believe that if you had had more time here and the matter had not broken upon you so suddenly, the declaration could have been composed n such a way that they would have caused less difficulties. While we cannot completely approve these statements, yet we have not lost confidence in the sincerity and affection of these brethren. A man may make a mistake and yet have the sincerest conviction and desire in his heart to do right. The Bible teaches us to exercise Christian charity and patience in such matters. I believe now that I have made known the feeling and attitude in America towards what happened in Europe. After all, we have the conviction that our brethren here take the non-combatant position also. We have spoken to brethren who went to the war and I can tell you that we did not find a greater military sprit among any of our brethren in Europe than in America. And I can also tell you that our brethren in Europe are as faithful in spirit and in their actions as our brethren in America. To express everything once again in other words: We regret some of the declaration which were sent out, but when we go back to the spirit and motives which led up to them, then we find that these brethren are standing as faithfully and sincerely to the work as are. And according to what should the individual be judged? Is it by the spirit or is it by the motives or is it by the declarations that are sent out? You will perhaps expect some declaration from the brethren who took up a contrary position on this question. Now we do not wish in any way to call in questions the intentions of the brethren who stand on the opposite side; we do not wish t judge the motives. But brethren during the time in which we studied the question in more detail, we came to the conviction that the course taken is not quite right. If the main motive in regard to non-combatancy had been right, nevertheless, according to our conviction which we gained over in America, the course followed is not quite... (the word was inaudible) ... Now we must say that each individual has had the right to form his own conviction and to make it a matter on conscience in regard to the war. And if you conscience does not allow you to put on a uniform, then it is your privileged to lay it off and you can stop at any place where you conscience tells you. But this must be a matter of conscience. When, however, you take your conscience as a standard and want to compel others to act according to your conscience, then you overstep your rights. In

America we said: Do not evade the law, be men, do not drawback from the call up, go to the government and tell them how you stand. I do not know of one case over there where anyone had evaded the mustering. There were men in the world over there who evaded the mustering and these are still being arrested and condemned. But I know of no Adventist who is being sought for today because he had evaded the mustering. A man who refused to put on the uniform on conscientious grounds, went straight to the government and said that he cannot wear the uniform. They answered him that he would go then to prison, upon which he replied, that he was ready to do so. That was the right position. Is it right form someone to evade the authorities? We further took the stand that no man, whatever kind of conscience he might have, should go so far as to make his conscience a standard for others. So we always believe that on this point opposition made a great mistake. We felt that during the war this point was a basis for waging war against their other brethren. It is bad enough that war should be among the nations, but when Christian wage war among themselves, it is much worse. Supposing that the documents which were sent out by the three brethren were wrong, what then? Let each live according to his conviction, and when the storm is over, then let us come together to express our views. It troubles us very much that such papers (from the Opposition Movement) were printed against our brethren at such a time. Brethren, it is a dangerous thing to do this. It calls forth a split too easily among the members who do not understand and grasp the situation. That calls forth a split in the church. And besides this, as long as the military laws are in force there still exists the great danger that the government will misunderstand us. We had to appear repeatedly before the government to explain our standpoint. We desired that the government should understand us. We had no fear regarding the consequences. We did not wish them, however, to misunderstand our position as citizen and Christians. But while all these documents were being printed and came even in the hands of the government, there was great danger that disaster would break upon the work. We have big institutions and interests in properties. Now when our fulfilment of duty demands that we relinquish them, then good, but we must know that we are doing our duty. And our brethren in America are of the opinion that it was not good to write these documents and distribute them and to bring all our institutions and establishments into danger. In America we had the same thing, but our brethren were very careful that nothing should be made public which would cause suspicion. The work was more important than personal views. I can live according to my conscience without waging war against me brethren. What I would like is to show the difference between someone who simply lives according to his conscience and someone who takes a belligerant position towards his brethren. We regretted these two things, first, the open opposition which arose against the brethren who had the leadership in their hands and then the publication and distribution of documents which were aimed at causing division among the brethren.

There is still another step which we believe is not right, and that is the formation of a separate organization to draw brethren (members) to itself and also the tithe and other offerings. We knew little about this till we came here and were informed. But that is no new principle which we had to consider and over which we had to decide. We have had opposition movements as long as our work has existed and men have always developed separate organizations in these opposition movements. In their efforts they have tried to draw in as many people as possible. They have tried to draw out as much money as possible from our churches. Our denomination has always opposed this matter and we ourselves as a people have never done this. It is true that we did come out of other churches and denominations, but how did we go out? Brethren, we went straight out and outside we created our own foundation. We never tried to take the meeting house or the monies of a denomination to which we belonged. I often heard Sister White speaking about this principle. It was in Australia. There were people who believe that the others were in error. They also believed that I was in error, and they decided to found an independent union in order to save the work. I was president of a field. When I learned about it they had already more or less drawn one whole church over their cause. They had also obliged the treasurer of the church to go out with the tithe. But we gathered the church together and explained the principles in question which were connected with it. By the grace of God there were more than a hundred who condemned this standpoint. Only fourteen people went with these two men. Sister

White was with us in Australia at that time. She went later with me to the church and this is the principle which she developed for us: Each one must follow his conviction and his conscience. If he cannot agree with the Adventist then he must go. But there is a right way to go. He can take his things and go and leave us in peace. Let them go and live out their own principles. She (Sister White) told how she and her husband went out of the Methodist church and how Joseph Bates left the Baptist church. When they received new light and their conscience no longer allowed them to remain there, they went out and waged no war and strife whatever in the denomination in which they had been up to then. They then developed for themselves their views as to how they should be taught. They began to build right from the bottom and they trusted in God to give them success if they were right. She then said thus: Brethren, never wage a conflict against those with whom you are connected. If you cannot walk together in peace with them, then withdraw. Now brethren, we regret very much. I do not want to speak in a condemnatory tone. I have also no bitter feelings in my heart, but if we could sit down and make it plain to the brethren who have been in this confrontation, then we would say: Brethren, you should not establish an organization among our people. You should not publish the papers and distribute them everywhere and then establish a new denomination in our own ranks in order to draw people out tithe and offerings from our people in this way. We as people have had to do pioneer work in this country. We in America have had to give thousands of dollars in order to take up the work here. The brethren have come over here to sacrifice their lives. None of you younger men have helped to establish the work. You received the truth from those who have done pioneer work and this organization is the work of those who labored here before and we regret it very much that this matter and this confusion has come upon us. (From now on Bro. Wentland translates.) Brethren, I do not want to take up too much time in speaking. I can stop at any time and begin again. But I think very seriously about these things and I am very concerned about them and I should like to throw light on this matter from many sides so that we may get to know it properly. Perhaps I should not say too much about it and should not dwell too long on it. I should perhaps now go over to the second question.

What proofs can be brought that they did not take the biblical course? I believe that I have already gone into this point rather thoroughly. Our denomination has the following principles according to which it acts in similar circumstances. It is also in harmony wit the counsel which Moses gave those who helped in the leadership of the work. There is a way to bring our matter before the brethren in order to be heard. Let us start with the church. Some members of the church may be somewhat offended about the officers or presidents. There may be something in the administration of a church with which they cannot agree. What should they do now? Should they immediately set up another church and separate? I say no. Bring you difficulties before the Field committee, and now let the brethren of the field committee know your matter. Now supposing that this is done and the members of the church concerned are not satisfied with the decision which was made, then they can go to the Union. Supposing they are satisfied with the decision of the Union, then they can go to the General Conference committee. We had a similar matter to settle in our spring session. A church brought a matter before the Field committee and also before the General Conference committee. The General Conference committee chose a committee from their midst which examined the matter and this committee then gave a report. This was thoroughly considered by the General Conference committee and also accepted. This report was then sent to the church. That is one way to settle our difficulties and one can say that in nine cases out of ten any further separation or difficulty is avoided. Supposing that the church refuses to accept the decision of the General Conference – it has a right to do this – then those in question must go. But they must withdraw in a Christian manner and leave us alone. They have this privilege. *But when they turn round to fight against us that does not show a Christian s spirit and can never prosper, and that is the reason that up to now no organization which took a position against us was able to stand. We have an experience of 75 years and I challenge anyone to name me a single movement that was able to coexist beside us after its followers had left us.* We do not say that someone who has left us is not able to lead a Christian life. I should not like to take that standpoint. But I will say this, *that no single organization could stand beside us.* They all came to an end. The brethren here in Germany as well as everywhere else had the privilege to appeal to the General Conference. The y had the privilege of formulating and expressing their views and to give the same explanation to the General Conference and we would certainly have given the mater our fullest attention. We would certainly have given the best advice which we could. And this could have happened in the greatest quietness without letting it come to a breakaway in our church, without bringing the members out of their course and without weakening their confidence and then we could have all remained together. But if it had then not been possible to work together, we could have separated in a Christian manner. Brothers and sisters, I know for certain through many years of experience what the position of the General Conference is concerning this matter. Had it been possible for us to speak to you right at the beginning about this difficulty, we would have said to you: However much brethren may have erred, be careful and quiet and commit it to the Lord and let Him care for it and do not let it come to a split. Do not fight against you brethren. Do not print or distribute any papers which could bring us and our institutions into difficulties. And when the storm and the difficulties are over, then we can come together and discuss this matter and arrive at a goal. That is the way we acted in America and the blessings of the Lord rests upon His people and because we held together the Lord blessed the work and it is going better now than ever before. With this I have answered the second question.

The next question is: Should we proclaim health reform in the future as the right arm of the message? Brethren, our position in regard to this health reform is the same today as it has ever been. Perhaps we are paying even more attention to this reform matter than ewe did formerly. We have a medical missionary department and have a secretary, Brother Hansen. He is laboring to organize this work in all churches better than only the food which we eat. This is really only a small part of the whole which we are endeavoring to lead forward. We have just now made new plans to bring the medical mission more into the missions. Brother Christian presented the matter before us in a certain manner when we were in Romania and he put it before the brethren here that if possible they should take four nurses there to instruct the peasants as to how they should live and to show them what right diet and general cleanliness is, and how everything should be done in accordance with health, to instruct them n the care of the body, on the treatment on infants and on contagious diseases and also as how mild illness can be treated. All these points are included in health reform. But also in this matter we must allow the spirit of love and tolerance to rue. We cannot exercise pressure or force upon members who do not do it as we wanted to do it. Many have a very limited view on health reform. They do not consider that there are various diseases in the human body. They do not consider the different countries, the geographical position, the scarcity of food and the difficulties. We believe in proper medical health reform as we have always done, and I believe that we shall make it a still stronger right arm than ever before. And we shall continue in this and when we have carried out this program so we shall be a greater blessing to the people than before.

I just notice that I have missed out part of the question: "What position does the General Conference take in regard to the Testimonies of Sister White? Are they inspired by God or not?" I am glad to be able to say that the General Conference has no changed its position toward the Testimonies in the last fifty years. If we have made any expressions in the sessions, nevertheless, we take the same standpoint as formerly. But I will say that individual persons may have changed their views about it. You well understand that the view of a single person can be somewhat different from that of the General Conference. We had people among us who had very extreme views. They were radical in both directions. But the General Conference has never take such a radical position. May I take a few minutes to show how they were radical in both directions. First: too much in favor of the *Testimonies*. There are some brethren among us who believe in a verbal inspiration. Hey have come so far that they believe in the infallibility of Sister White. I know of some brethren who, when they read something from her *Testimonies*, wrote it down and put it on the same level as the Bible. I know of people who studied her writings right through, that is to say personally, and then wrote her answers in a book and then considered these words as the Bible. I know people who placed these two things, the Bible and the *Testimonies*, beside each other and appreciated them equally. The

General Conference has never done this and has never made a resolution which would prove this. She herself (Sister White) never claimed such a thing. Nor did she ever maintain that when she wrote her books or held an address that her words were inspired. She always warned people not to accept her answers as the final decision. Some people who took such a radical position towards the *Testimonies* have now take up a more moderate position. I will not linger too long upon this. But I will say that the position concerning the *Testimonies* remains as it has been up to now. (Bro. Kern said: "And more of her books are sold now in he church than ever before.") I should like to go more deeply into this question, and that before all, if we should have time before all our work. In the worker's meetings all over the world we said: We should like to present the absolute truth about the Testimonies and the person of Sister White. We all know that the Lord called her to this position when He began the work, and I believe there are few Seventh-day Adventists in the world who would question this. The difficulties which some have, come about in this way: these brethren interpret the Testimonies after their manner and want to force others to accept their interpretation and thus difficulties arise. These are the greatest difficulties which I had concerning the *Testimonies* in the last 25 years. I can well accept them as they are; but the manner in which some want to interpret them, this bring me difficulties.

The fourth question: "Is the message national or international?" We have read the statement in the *Zion's Watchman* of March 1920. Brethren, it is really no question whatever for this denomination. If we believe anything, then we believe that it is a worldwide message for all nations and languages. We find that what the mentioned *Zion's Watchman* says is in no way different from this. In the sentence which has been read nothing can be found which would make the cause a national one. We understand the contrary. The history of the Reformation movement always shows that the Lord calls out people from all over the world to the light. People in England, France, Germany and everywhere, equally pious and devoted have been led by God to the light. The cause did not only begin in Germany, it did not have its central point in England only. God awakened a Wycliffe but also called Luther and pious men in France. Thus it was in our movement, this it was in 1844. At that time light penetrated into various lands, but it came in a kind of flood upon America. The movement itself, however, is worldwide and international. It seems to me as if my conscience was saying that I should now stop. I consider it to me a great privilege that I could speak to you and present these principles before you. I admit that I have done somewhat imperfectly. If I have made the tome and the strength to write it down and to read it to you, it would have turned out better. It would have been weighed better, but time did not allow it. I have been almost the whole year on journeys from one place to another and I have had meetings always from morning till evening. I have little rest and after 20 years of labor I cannot bear so much as formerly. But I am glad of the good spirit which has prevailed in this deliberation. I do not wish to say one word which would wound the heart of anyone. I know that my opinions differ from those of some who are here present. What I have said here may not be acceptable to everyone but I have tried to present the views of my brethren and I know that they are sincere. I hope that the good Spirit of God will lead us to unity. We need not be surprised that is has also disconcerted us a little. But brethren, (to the Opposition Movement) we should be very conciliatory and try to come back to the right way. Now we cannot share this opinion with you that our denomination is on the wrong way. We also cannot share the opinion tat our denomination is Babylon. We do not admit this for a minute. (This sentence is spoken with special emphasis.) We cannot admit that all our members in all countries and fields have departed from the right way.

*M.E. Kern:* Sister White once reproved a brother very decidedly who maintained in America at that time that our denomination was Babylon. *

---

* Bro. Kern means a certain brother Garmire [sic] to whom sister White addressed an open letter at that time which was published in the *Review and Herald* of September 12, 1893, and in which the following can be read:

"My brother, I heard that you take the position that the Seventh-day Adventist church is Babylon and that all who wish to be saved must go out of it. You are not the only one whom the enemy has mislead on this point. For the last 40 years, one man after the other has arisen and has maintained that the Lord has sent him with the same message; but let me tell you, as I have told them, that the message which you proclaim is one of the satanic deceptions intended to cause confusion among the churches. My brother, you have surely left the right road... If you teach that the Seventh-day Adventist church is Babylon, you are in error. God has given you no such message."

*A.G. Daniells:* The numerous persons have arisen who maintained that we were Babylon and have called, "Come out!" We have a tract, written by Sister White, n which she warns of this and says, we may make mistakes, but the Lord has chosen His people, and He says: This is my precious possession in the world. And if He has led them out He will not forsake them. He will try them and sanctify them and purify them, but He will never reject the remnant of His people. Our opinion is that here in this case it is a great mistake to maintain such a thing in spite of the fact that we are prepared to admit that we are fallible men. Bro. Dail has often said to me: Bro. Daniells. I wish I had not sent out my statement! And he is a Christian man and fears God. He is ready to sacrifice everything and to live for the Lord and no for himself. We are prepared to admit that we are fallible and can err, but we cannot admit for one minute that we (to say, as a denomination) have turned from the right way and that another movement must take our place. We maintain that we are still on the original path of this work. Perhaps you can still remember the vision which Sister White had concerning an iceberg and a steamer sailing on the sea which meets the iceberg and then sinks. That is what she saw in a vision concerning such movements. Then [she saw] a reversed relation. She saw the ship tremble from one end to another as it struck the iceberg and she saw how it then again reregained its balance and sailed on and finally entered the harbor. [That is to say, the iceberg, in this case, represents such opposition movements, the ship represents the church. While, in the other case, the ship sinks and the iceberg swims on, the opposite happens in this case: the iceberg (Opposition Movement) melts or sinks, but the ship (church) reaches harbor.]* She told this to me in a time of crisis and great difficulties and said, "Brother Daniells, sound an encouraging note everywhere in the whole world. We will enter the harbor." This is our position in the whole world. We should all humble our hearts before God and try to do right and to act right. We should never be ashamed to confess where we have erred, but brethren, it is the greatest of all mistakes to separate ourselves from the work, to organize a new movement and to try

---

* The statement within brackets appears in the original. - EDITOR

to carry through such a thing. I tell you it can only bring confusion and finally it must perish and those who were connected with it will come back or remain lying by the way. Therefore we say: Let us go forward together. Bro Spicer's last words to me in America were, "You will be seeing the brethren in Germany, hen bring them back. Bring about a reconciliation if possible." Nevertheless, he stands firm in relation to the movement, and while he admits that technical mistakes (that is to say, mistakes in the handling of our principles) have been committed on the part of the brethren, yet I firmly believe that the brethren of the opposition side have committed fundamental mistakes (that is to say, offenses against the principles of truth). This circumstance would destroy and overthrow the whole thing even if they were right regarding questions of practice. My prayer is that we shake hands and be reconciled now that the war is over. May the Lord help us to do this. Amen.

I believe that we should offer an earnest prayer to the Lord before we close. We are here and have a great work to do, but we have a great enemy who seeks to bring us destruction. Christ is our only hope and we should ask Him to help us before we close.

Prayer: Bro. Paul Drinhaus.

Adjourned.

## VI. Session. Friday, July 23, 1920, 7 0'clock in the morning

Present: All members of the last session (full meeting). Prayer: Bro. J Muth.

Interpreter: Bro. W.C. Ising

*A.G. Daniells:* We have assembled together in order that the brethren (of the Opposition Movement) may have an opportunity to reply yesterday's meeting. We will time no time for an introduction but will give them an opportunity at once.

*E. Doerschler:* We have come there as representatives of the people and have presented four questions to the brethren. We had still more questions but yesterday evening we had these four answered. Now first of all I must still ask a question which can perhaps be answered briefly. Is this the final answer of the General Conference?

*A.G. Daniells:* Should an answer be given to this?

*E. Doerschler:* Yes.

*A.G. Daniells:* I do not know properly how this is to be understood.

*E. Doerschler:* Whether Brother Daniells passed the final decision of the entire General Conference committee yesterday?

*A.G. Daniells:* I think, brethren, that we had to give this judgment as far as we are concerned. I am trying to say that this means that the matter could not be discussed in a larger session. I do not wish to be hard and to break of the matter at once. As far as our conviction and our judgment goes, as far as we are concerned, we believe that is our final judgement.

*E. Doerschler:* Is there a higher authority?

*A.G. Daniells:* There is no higher authority, at the most, a larger number of brethren. In our Autumn meeting we will have a larger number of brethren who will assembly together. But it would only be a body of these members of the General Conference committee.

*E. Doerschler:* We regret very much that we did not ask this yesterday evening. We like to be very careful in these things also. I for my part judge at this moment that we should wait with our final decision till the time when more brethren (a larger numbers of members) can judge this matter.

*A.G. Daniells:* How do you want to present the matter before a larger body there in Washington?

*E. Doerschler:* Again through a representation. We have heard that a meeting is t take lace in Switzerland again.

*A.G. Daniells:* It should be just the same body as here. There will be no further persons in addition to those that are here, only Brethren Spicer and Knox will come over from America.

*E. Doerschler:* Would it not be very important for brethren to come together from the whole world for this final decision? For we must consider that this then would prevent a conflict to the utmost.

*A.G. Daniells:* Brethren, we have such an ample experience in all the steps which you have taken in separating yourselves from the main body. You have waged a conflict with the body as whole, a special conflict. We have gone through everything in detail so that we have a good knowledge of the standpoint of each individual. I am sure that the brethren (of the General Conference committee) would pronounce the same judgment as we have doe yesterday evening. As regards the differences of opinion and motives by which you have allowed yourselves t be led, it might be that they would pay more attention to this point. But this we have also tried to do here with the greatest care. But regarding the whole course which you have taken, we are clear what it means to the denomination. I spoke about this in detail to Bro. Spicer. He was here at the time. He said: We can never allow this, for it is contrary to the whole history of our denomination. We have counseled about this matter repeatedly and can never give our consent to it, and I am certain that this would be the answer of all our brethren. I believe we should not lose either time or money to give you false hopes in regard to the outcome of the matter. We are not disturbed with regard to a conflict to the utmost. We have often gone through such difficulties and the opposition has always come to a very sad end. A few years ago we had a matter in Serbia, but when we brought the whole affair before the delegation, 35 of the 75 members who were present left. The rest remained. We are not worried about this, but what we regret is the loss of members. We do not wish to see any human wrecks, not more than is absolutely necessary. We do not want to refuse the possibility of calling together a larger body, but we wish to tell you that the matter can take no other course by this. In this case we would also wish you to send your documents and letters instead of your coming to Washington.

*Spanknoebel:* Dear Brethren, you see by our presence here and the discussions, that it is our sincere wish to proclaim the message in unity. Because of this we made a proposal before we separate completely from the whole denomination. The responsibility for what will follow rests on you. But we want to say a brief word about this declaration, and this can either further our proposal to you or bring a refusal. Our hearts are very moved at this hour. We wish to follow Jesus, we wish to be saved and to help others through this message. Now I should like to reply briefly to the four questions which were answered yesterday: We asked: How do the brethren of the General Conference stand concerning the 4th and 6th commandments wit reference to the war question? The different counsels here and in America testify that there was no complete clarity among the Advent people on this question until the wartime. We have a positive message for God and this message regulates all our relations to the authorities and saves us into the kingdom of glory. Now, if a position were taken against the sixth commandment in Germany but not in America, it is not possible for both to be right. The law of God can be understood by anyone who wants to understand it, both great and small. It is a revelation of God. Now, if the problem were so great that it would need perhaps decade of experience, then it would be impossible for u to proclaim the message of God. We believe that we, in order to follow Jesus at this time according to the Scriptures and the *Testimonies*, cannot go to war. We allow liberty of conscience to everyone. In heaven there is also liberty of conscience, but not a liberty of conscience which overthrows the principles of the law of God. We find now that the brethren in America allowed liberty of conscience to such an extent that the law of God was transgressed. In Germany there was open violation of the law, and the brethren in America understood that that is not right, and now we do not know why the decision was made in this way or in that way. Here are now brethren who, through earnest prayer, have received clearness from the Lord. Here are brethren who have spent three years in prison for the Lord. Some have died in prison and have given a good testimony for Jesus. Should not our message continue to educate such soldiers of the cross? But when is that possible? The message must be proclaimed in all its precision so that a peculiar people, a united people may fight and be victorious under the banner of the Lord. We are thankful to God that we can have certainty in this message and we believe that in the coming storms and difficulties, in order to be able to stand and to be united with Christ or King, we must fight under His banner and encourage others to do the same. Now if we proclaim the law of God as it is in Christ, many will prepare themselves for the conflict. But if we continue along this road as in the past, we will be an unprepared people in the coming storms. Now we wish to follow our Saviour further in the way in which I have stated regarding this point

Now regarding the second point, when the decision against the law of God was made in Germany and various brethren were disfellowshiped from the body because of their conscience, we had to continue on our way with this message according to our conviction, and the fact that we held repeated meetings to discuss these important things is proof that he biblical way has been adhered to and we as a people are justified before God and the church. That now in this movement many people arose with erroneous teachings and fanaticism, this is very regrettable and where we as men have made mistakes we want to ask all brethren and sisters to forgive us. But we cannot depart from this way upon which the Lord has placed us and we feel a burden to proclaim this message. We would very willingly hand over this responsibility to someone else but we can do no other. We must proclaim it.

Now with regard to the third question, we believe concerning the *Testimonies*, that they are inspired by God. Regarding these things Sister White writes that there is no half way. The *Testimonies* are either from God or from the devil. We believe that they are from God. We do not place them above the Bible but we heed and obey what she (Sister White) says. We do not idolize the person. She was only an instrument and her words are inspired by God. Through heeding her words we can attain sanctification in Christ. By this message the Lord will gather a united people from all nations, and He is gathering this people and in His grace He wishes to give us a share in it. We cannot complete the work, but He will do it in a wonderful manner, and we rust in Him, and if only a few of us are standing here, then we can only say that we can do no other and may the Lord help us. We are not hostile towards you brethren because of this today. We want to part as friends. We do not wish to fight against you but desire to use the liberty which God has given us for our salvation and for the saving of souls, and may the Lord give us grace that when Jesus comes in the cloud of heaven He may be our king and we may enter in with Him. This is our desire for us all. Amen.

*E. Doerschler:* I am thankful to God that I can inform you that we as representatives of the people were of one heart and of one mind. We knew that in the future we must carry the message unitedly, hand in hand, also regarding the fourth commandment, the Sabbath, which was transgressed during the four years and is also transgressed today. [We knew] that it shall be proclaimed more fully, as Sister White also writes that the Sabbath shall be proclaimed more fully and we should like to act in accordance with Isa. 8:20,21 which says, "To the law and to the testimony: if they speak not according to this word, it is because there is not light in them. And they shall pass through it, hardly bestead and hungry: and it shall come to pass, that when they shall be hungry, they shall fret themselves, and curse their king and their God, and look upward." The other class is meant by this. Amen

*A.G. Daniells:* (after a short recess): Brethren, I am extremely sorry that you are not inclined to follow the counsel which the brethren who have much experience have given you. I feared that you would not. It is very rare for brethren who have taken such a course to accept such counsels. In general, these appeals which are to us are not made to obtain our advice, but mostly only to obtain our concessions and our consent, and when this is impossible for us, the naturally a separation takes place. But we always take time to examine openly, carefully and with patience the matter that the brethren put before us. We believe that you are completely in error in the views which you represent. We believe in the fourth commandment just as much as we have always done, but we are not in the position to agree with your interpretation of it. What you have said about Moses, if, after the law had been given from Sinai, he had commanded you a few days later to kill the king of Bashan and all men and women and children. Would you have accused him of murder? But God commanded him to transgress the sixth commandment. You see that there are many things to be found in the interpretation of the commandments, and we must have liberty to read and understand the commandments and not to be bound to the way some small body may interpret them. Now regarding the counsel of Sister White and the position which the brother (turning to Spanknoebel) takes: Now, brother, I believe that if you have only half the faith that you profess to have in the *Testimonies*, then you would have ceased long ago to belong to this Opposition Movement. I cannot think that you have studied her advice concerning unity and the danger and the mistake which lies in separating. If you would follow the advice given by her, then you would need many years before undertaking such a separation. It is just this apparatus which has been organized together with Sister

White which had led to the denomination holding together. I was a young man at the time when the division began.* It also happened in our conference in which I was. The president and secretary were at the head of this apostate movement. Brother and Sister White hastened to get there and she presented before them the warning which the Lord ha given her against this movement. And two thirds of the conference were then on their side. But first Sister White had stood alone there with a small minority, and I tell you also in the name of the Lord that you will not go through. These apostate movements are not of God and you will certainly not be able to stand. Those people at that time did not want to accept the counsel. They felt that they had to go on. I believe that not a hundred remain of those who were connected with it, but the small minority of that time today numbers three thousand in the conference. And thus it has happened repeatedly. Separations began already in the time of Moses. On he part of the children of God mistakes always have been made. We are all fallible, and

---

*[In this translation, we give the quotation in the footnote as it appeared in the original English publication, rather than from the German language edition. – EDITOR] "During the fall of 1853 a few disaffected ones in Michigan joined together and began the publication of a sheet called the Messenger of Truth. The mission of this sheet and its conductors seemed to be to tear down and defame instead of to build up. Many falsehoods were inserted in its pages, which annoyed us in our work in the message; and as it was our first experience with such an open attack, we thought it our duty to refute their slanderous statements. Doing this occupied time that should have been spent in advancing the truth committed to our trust, and suited well the purposes of Satan, who was undoubtedly the instigator of this opposition. And thus the state of affairs continued until the evening of June 20, 1855, when Elder White and his wife, Elder Cottrell, and myself had just closed a meeting in Oswego, N.Y. We had been annoyed in our meeting by one Lillis, who came in and circulated those slanderous documents among the people. Again the question as to our duty in this matter came up. All previous efforts at answering their falsehoods had only resulted in their manufacturing more.

"At a prayer-meeting held that evening at the house of John Place, in the city of Oswego, Mrs. White was given a vision in which she was shown that if we would keep at our work, preaching the truth, regardless of any such people as the "Messenger party," they would go to war among themselves and their paper would go down, and when that should happen we would find that our ranks had doubled. Believing this testimony to be from the Lord, we began at once to act in harmony with it.

"The cause of truth advanced rapidly, while the "Messenger party" got into trouble among themselves. In a brief space of time the party were scattered, many of their leaders having given up the Sabbath..." – J.N. Loughborough, *The Great Second Advent Movement*, pp. 325,326

those who only wish to point out certain mistakes and errors can well do so. But they do not form a reason for separation. They did the same with Moses formerly but without success. God calls for unity and therefore we should settle our difficulties together. But separation does not settle the difficulty. I sincerely beg you not to follow a false course, a false conception and a false light. Do not do this. I know exactly this morning what the result of this course will be what it will be after ten years if the Lord has not come by then. The controversial question among us was this: You want that we, as brethren of the General Conference should give our seal of consent to your machinations. That would lead to our supporting all the efforts for division in the whole world. But that would bring us away from the foundation of our denomination. It would cause a thousand of such divisions. Some time ago I received a letter from one of your brethren I believe he said in it that about 15 different bodies have been formed from those who went away at that time. That is what it always leads to and you will have more and more of it. You will always Disfellowship more people from you and finally the whole thing will be dispersed like water in the sand. Brethren, do not take such a course. Give your full attention to this matter; say like Ruth, "Thy God is my God, and thy people shall be my people; whither thou goest, I will go." I beg you to take this course. But if you believe that you are not able to do so, then you are free to go your own way and we shall have to appeal to our own selves. We shall explain our standpoint and our position to our people and will have to safeguard them. Naturally, we cannot sit still inactive without informing our members of the result of this council here. For we cannot allow any to come into our churches brethren and to bring about a separation movement without giving an admonition ad warning about it. Some months ago I spoke already to a party who had also caused a separation – it had nothing to do with the military question – and I said to them: If you want to go away then we can do nothing against it, and if you go out quietly and stand on your on foundation you will not hear anything from us, and we will not pursue you to your disadvantage. We shall not make any public statement, but if you continue your propaganda in our churches and if you produce literature and try to distribute it in our churches, then you will hear from us. We will not make difficulties for anyone who goes away from us in a quiet manner. But we will never sit still and allow people to enter into our churches without our giving warning. We do not want to be enemies and I pray to God that He may lead us in His ways.

Hamburg, September 9, 1920.
R. Ruehling, Secretary